Learn to Cook
Potatoes

John Fenton-Smith

HARLAXTON

Page 2: Greek style Potato Salad makes a lovely luncheon dish or an accompaniment to a barbecue or any outdoor meal. The preparation is shown on the endpapers.

Published by
Harlaxton Publishing Limited
2 Avenue Road, Grantham, Lincolnshire, NG31 6TA
United Kingdom
A Member of the Weldon International Group of Companies

First Published in 1994

Publisher: Robin Burgess
Project Coordinator: Barbara Beckett
Designer: Rachel Rush
Editor: Alison Leach
Illustrator: Maggie Renvoize
Photographer: Rodney Weidland
Food styling assisted by John Fenton-Smith
Produced by Barbara Beckett Publishing
Colour Separation: G.A. Graphics, Stamford, UK
Printer: Imago, Singapore

British Library Cataloguing-in-Publication data.
A catalogue record for this book is available from the British Library

Title: Learn to Cook, POTATOES
ISBN: 1 85837 088 4

Cook's Notes 6
Measurements and Ingredients

Introduction 8

Boiling 10
*Sweet Potato Soup 10 • Potato and Carrot Soup 12 • Basic Potato Salad 13
Vinaigrette Dressing 13 • Minty Potato Salad 14 • Hot Potato Salad 14 • Country Salad 15
Sweet Potato and Coconut Pudding 16*

Steaming 17
*Caramelized Potatoes 17 • Greek-Style Potato Salad 18 • Sweet Potato Pancakes 19
Potato Scones 20*

Mashing 22
*Mashed Potato 22 • Potato and Onion Soup 27 • Mashed Potato and Thyme Soup 27
Potato and Carrot Casserole 28 • Mashed Potatoes with Cream 30
Curried Potato Patties 30 • Chocolate Potato Cake 31 • Potato Cream 31*

Baking 32
*Baked Stuffed Potato 33 • Baked Potatoes Italian Style 33
Sweet Potato Purée 34 • Oven-Baked Potato Chips (French Fries) 34 • Gruyère Potatoes 35
Baked Potatoes French Style 35 • Crunchy Baked Potato Skins 36 • Irish Stew 36*

Roasting 38
Unpeeled Roast Potatoes 38 • Crispy Little Roast Potatoes 38 • Hasselbach Potatoes 40

Sautéing and Shallow-Frying 41
*Sautéed Lemon Potatoes 41 • Veal with Potatoes 42 • Spiced Potatoes 42
Hashed Brown Potatoes 44*

Deep-Frying 45
Potato Croquettes 45 • Basic Potato Chips (French Fries) 46 • Herb and Potato Balls 47

Glossary 48

Measurements

All spoon and cup measurements are level. Standard spoon and cup measures are used in all the recipes. I recommend using a graduated nest of measuring cups: 1 cup, ½ cup, ⅓ cup and ¼ cup. The graduated nest of spoons comprises 1 tablespoon, 1 teaspoon, ½ teaspoon and ¼ teaspoon. For liquids, use a standard litre or imperial pint measuring jug which also shows cup measurements. As the metric/imperial/US equivalents given are not exact, follow only one system of measurement within the recipe.

Ovens should be preheated to the specified temperature. When cooking in a saucepan or frying pan (skillet), use a moderate heat unless directed otherwise.

Ingredients

There are over 300 **potato** varieties recognized around the world today. As it is impossible in a book of this size to refer to even most of them, I have referred to types such as waxy or floury (mealy as it is known in some countries) and you should look for these qualities among local brand names, whatever the season. **Herb** quantities are for fresh herbs; if fresh are unobtainable, use half the quantity of dried herbs. Use freshly ground black **pepper** whenever pepper is listed; use **salt** and pepper to individual taste. Use plain (all-purpose) **flour** unless otherwise stated. **Oils** used include cold-pressed virgin olive oil and corn or peanut (groundnut) oil for flavour; otherwise sunflower oil is recommended rather than other 'vegetable' oils. Use unsalted **butter**. Granulated **sugar** is used unless otherwise stated. Some recipes call for chicken **stock**. A prepared form in cubes or powders, which are then dissolved in water, can be obtained in most supermarkets.

Sweet Potato and Coconut Pudding (p. 16) is a truly outstanding dessert with a difference. Sweet and spicy with citrus overtones.

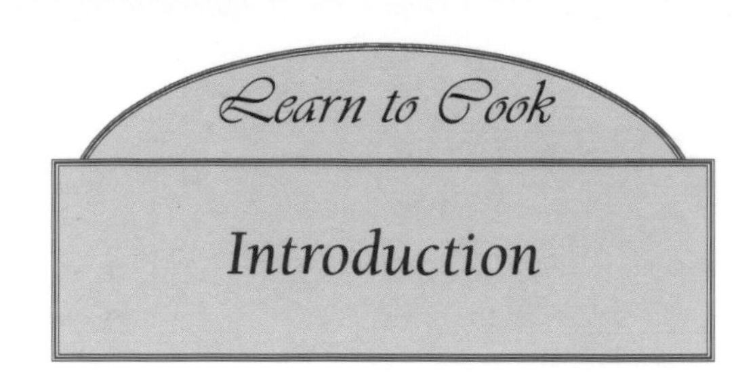

The humble potato is one of our most delicious vegetables. It comes from South America and is one of the oldest cultivated vegetables known. It was a staple item in the diet of the ancient Incas at least 8000 years ago and is now one of the world's four largest food crops, standing alongside rice, wheat and corn. The potato started its long journey to our tables from South America to Europe about the time of Queen Elizabeth I. It was quickly embraced by Ireland and then spread to other places on the continent and so to other parts of the world in the wake of European expansion.

Potatoes can be boiled, steamed, fried, baked or roasted, mashed, or partly cooked and frozen. They can be served as entrées, accompaniments or as main dishes by themselves, or even marvellous desserts! There are a number of delicious salads that can be made from potatoes. Salads come in many shapes and forms and each country has its own variations.

This book will teach you how to cook potatoes even if you have never cooked before. It explains the basic steps as well as cooking techniques you may not have tried before or feel a little nervous about trying.

The instructions are clearly set out. There are step-by-step guides to the different cooking methods, such as steaming, roasting and sautéing. Many recipes are photographed in preparation to show a special technique as well as what the finished dish looks like and how to present it for the table. Detailed step-by-step drawings also illustrate dicing vegetables, making potato chips (French fries); or making potato scones. There are handy hints set off in boxes, giving information such as how to prevent discolouration, choose between waxy and floury potatoes, and how to make extra crispy chips.

A glossary of cooking terms is on page 48 for you to look up any term that is unfamiliar. There is a list of recipes on page 5 for your reference. Be sure to read the information on measurements and ingredients on page 6.

One of the most important things to do when trying a new recipe is to read the recipe very thoroughly before starting. Check that you have all the ingredients, and make an estimate of the amount of time needed. Have you time to make a sophisticated recipe like Herb and Potato Balls or would it be better to simply mash or roast the potatoes?

Potatoes were once thought to be a fattening vegetable but they are, in fact, almost 80 per cent water and contain a lot of vitamins and minerals that are important to a healthy diet. Most of these substances are located just below or even in the skin so it is a good idea to cook potatoes in their jackets whenever possible.

The greater part of the vitamins and minerals are Vitamin C and iron, but the potato also contributes potassium to our diet, which counters salt intake. Salt, of course, is considered by many medical experts to be a major contributor to high blood pressure and heart disease.

Whichever method of cooking you use, careful preparation is important. Discard any potatoes that have green patches and remove all the eyes where sprouting occurs, as well as bruised or cut areas caused by excessive handling and coarse harvesting procedures. If you must peel them (remember, many of the nutrients are in the skin), do so evenly and not too deeply. Small new potatoes only need gentle wiping with damp paper towels.

When proportioning your food amongst guests, follow these simple guidelines. One single serving per person is the equivalent of four small new potatoes or one medium-sized old potato or one small sweet potato.

Potatoes can bruise, so when buying and storing, handle them as carefully as possible. When buying potatoes, choose ones that are firm, dry and sprout-free, and have no green spots. The green spots appear where potatoes are exposed to light and they contain poisonous alkalords. Store them in a dry, cool, darkened space where the air can circulate freely. Dampness only leads to mouldiness and rot, and warmth leads to sprouting. Never keep them in a polythene bag—always remove them as soon as you get home from the supermarket—and never store them near strong-smelling food such as onions.

'Old' and 'new' are terms often applied to potatoes. The terms describe their age, not their type. Old potatoes are last year's crop and new come from the current season's harvest. With new potatoes, size, variety and type (waxy or floury) are irrelevant. Freshly dug new potatoes are usually much sweeter than their older relations because the sugar has not yet turned to starch. The potato skin is also not fully developed so will be flaky and can be removed easily when rubbed with the thumb.

There are hundreds of varieties of potato and brand names will differ from country to country, although fewer than fifteen would be available in any one place. Your choices are mostly limited to red or white skinned potatoes. The flesh can be white and creamy, yellow and firm, soft and waxy, dry or floury and textures in between. Mealy fleshed potatoes are the dry types which contain more starch than waxy varieties and are therefore better suited to baking and mashing, but useless for boiling as they fall apart when cooking.

There is also the sweet potato. While not strictly a potato, it also is a native of South America as well as the West Indies and the Pacific. The skin can be pinkish or light milk coffee-coloured and it has a nobbly, long shape. The flesh can be bright orange, yellowish or white. Used much the same way as the potato, it is often cooked as a dessert because of its relatively high—3–6 per cent—sugar content. Compared to a white potato, sweet potato provides more calories, minerals and vitamin A, but less protein.

No special equipment is needed for cooking potatoes though it is handy to have an old-fashioned potato masher for mashing. Very sharp knives, and a range of them, are a necessity in any kitchen. Saucepans and frying pans (skillets) are far more efficient if they have thick, heavy metal bases and tight-fitting lids. The thick base ensures even cooking and retention of heat. It is worthwhile investing in a food processor if you are serious about cooking, because it saves so much time and energy.

Well now, enjoy yourself and good cooking!

Boiling is one of the oldest and most efficient cooking techniques. The whole surface of the vegetable is in contact with boiling water at a constant temperature of 100°C/212°F. A potato can be boiled in less time than it takes to bake at double the temperature!

For flavoursome, whole boiled potatoes, you need ones that won't break up during cooking. Firm, waxy, white or yellowish flesh is best. A waxy potato contains less starch and more liquid than other types, which means it will keep its shape and absorb less water while cooking. It is therefore ideal to use in soups and salads. If the potato is to be mashed after boiling, then a floury or mealy variety should be used.

To boil potatoes whole, cover the vegetable with water, bring to the boil, then turn down to simmer for 20–30 minutes, depending on the size of the potatoes. New potatoes should be put into boiling water and old ones brought to the boil in the water. When the potato can be pierced right through by a thin bamboo or metal skewer, remove from the heat, drain well, and if not served immediately, cover with a clean cloth (not a lid) so that excess moisture is absorbed and the potato becomes dry and floury, not sodden.

Boiled new potatoes can be eaten skin and all. Old potatoes should be boiled with the skin intact, then peeled by holding in a dry tea-towel (dish cloth). As a variation to enrich the flavour of the potato, use stock or milk instead of water. Nutrients in potatoes dissolve less readily in milk and they will taste sweeter than usual. Remember to keep the milk just simmering so that it doesn't scorch or curdle. Once the potatoes are cooked, the liquid can be used to make a soup or cream sauce.

Sweet Potato Soup

900 g/2 lb sweet potatoes, peeled and cut into dice
900 ml/1½ pints /3¾ cups water
1 onion, thinly sliced
1 tablespoon sunflower oil
250 ml/8 fl oz/1 cup plain yoghurt
½ teaspoon salt, if liked
1 tablespoon finely chopped parsley, to garnish
1 tablespoon grated orange peel, to garnish

Cook the sweet potatoes in the water until tender. Sauté the onion in the oil until transparent. Purée the potatoes, liquid and onion in batches until smooth. Return the purée to the pan and stir in the yoghurt and salt and reheat gently. Serve garnished with the parsley and orange.
Serves 6

A Country Salad (p. 15) adds brightness to the table if you use different coloured peppers (capsicums, bell peppers) when in season.

Potatoes not only have different types of flesh but also come in a variety of shapes, size and colour.

Potato and Carrot Soup

A simple soup to make, the carrots add a lively dash of colour. Use waxy potatoes that will keep their shape.

2 tablespoons sunflower oil
1 small onion, cut into dice
5 carrots, cut into dice
2 firm or waxy potatoes, cut into dice
1.15 litres/2 pints/5 cups water
Salt and pepper
1 teaspoon chopped marjoram
1 teaspoon paprika
¼ teaspoon sugar

Heat the oil in a pot, add the onion and sauté for 2 minutes. Add the carrots and cook for a further 3 minutes. Add the potatoes and the water and simmer for 1 hour or until the vegetables are tender. Season with salt, pepper, marjoram, paprika and sugar.
Serves 4

Potato stock. *Do not throw out potato water once you have boiled the vegetable as it contains lots of vitamins and minerals extracted from the skin. Use the water to cook other vegetables or as a soup stock.*

Basic Potato Salad

It is necessary for the potato to keep its shape in a salad, so select the firm, waxy variety.

900 g/2 lb potatoes
125 ml/4 fl oz/½ cup mayonnaise
4 tablespoons vinaigrette dressing
½ teaspoon sugar
2 tablespoons chopped parsley
3 shallots, chopped
Salt and pepper, if liked

Cook the unpeeled potatoes in boiling water for 20 minutes. Drain and when cool enough to handle, peel and cut into cubes or slices. Combine the remaining ingredients in a bowl, add the potatoes and toss lightly.
Serves 6

Vinaigrette Dressing
125 ml/4 fl oz/½ cup olive oil
2 tablespoons vinegar
1 teaspoon prepared mustard, if liked
1 tablespoon mixed herbs
Salt and pepper

Stir all the ingredients together until thoroughly combined, or place them in a small screw-topped jar and shake vigorously.
Makes ¾ cup

Dicing Vegetables

Potato strips are cut into 12 mm/½ inch cubes.

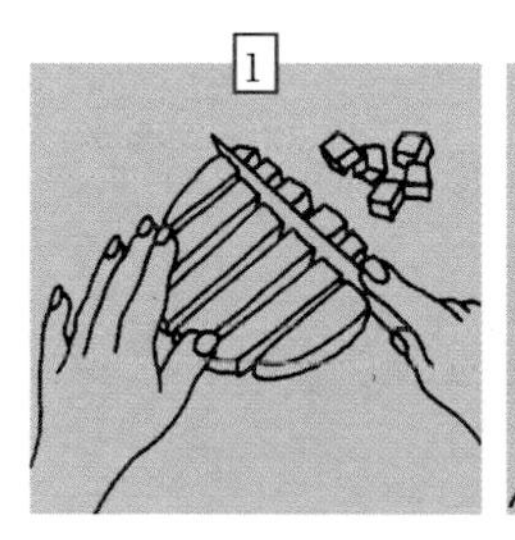

Cut sweet potatoes into even-sized chunks.

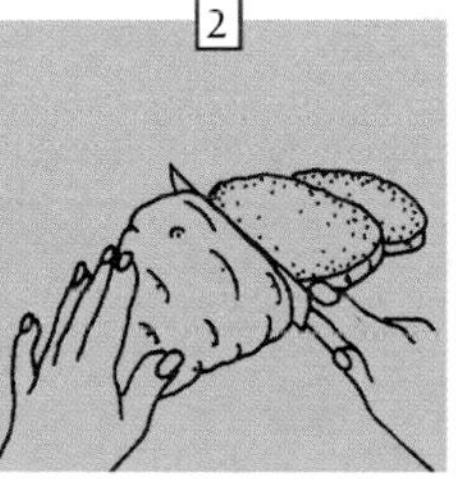

Cut onions into thin slices before dicing.

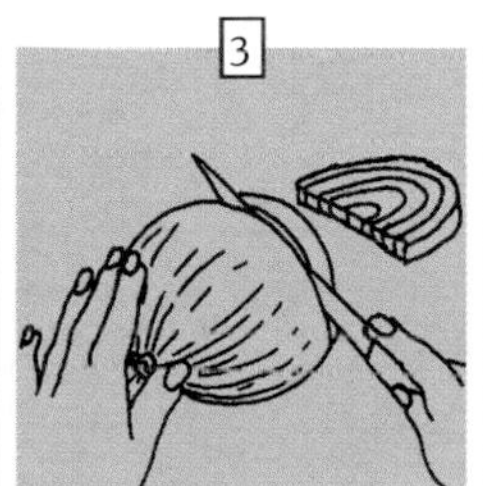

Carrots are cut into rings across the width of the vegetable.

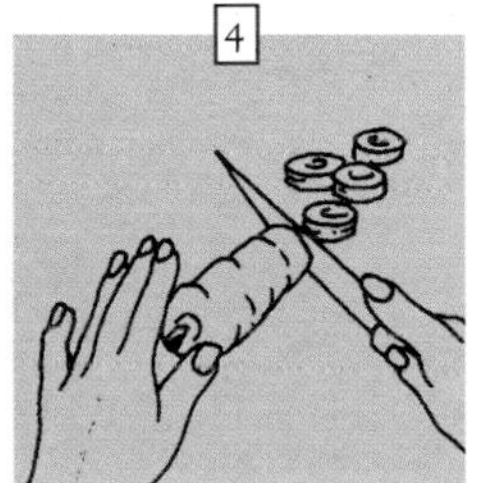

Preparing Peppers (Capsicums, Bell Peppers) and Sieving Eggs

Cut off stalk end of pepper. Remove central core and ribs.

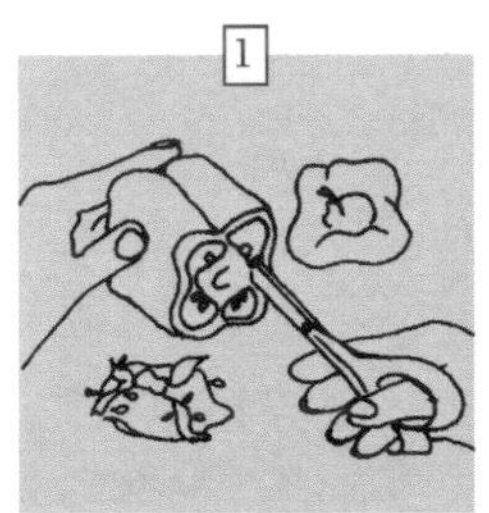

Slice pepper across its width to form rings.

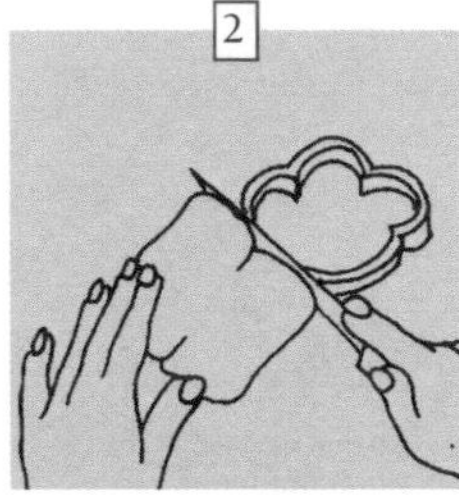

Hard-boiled egg is cut along its length into even-sized circles.

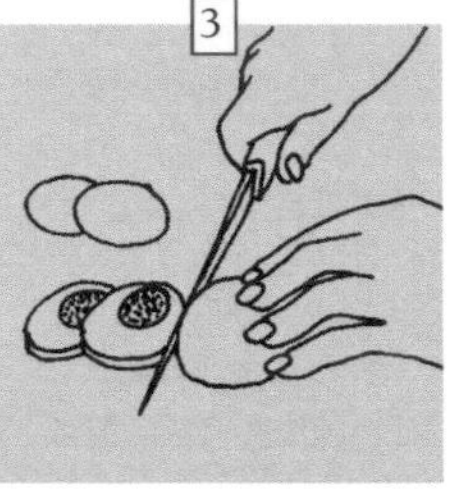

Press egg slices through a sieve.

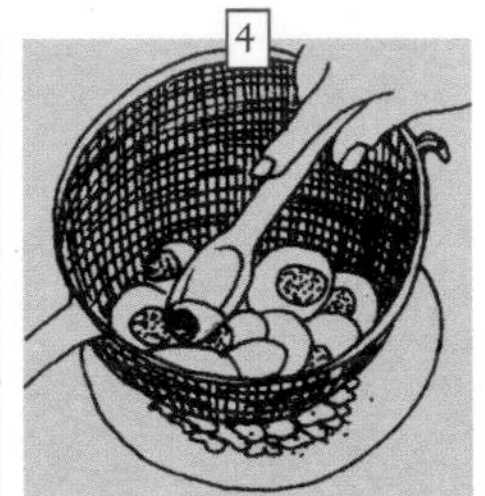

Minty Potato Salad

2 litres/3½ pints/2¼ quarts stock
900 g/2 lb potatoes
3 tablespoons mint sprigs

Bring the stock to the boil in a large saucepan, add the potatoes and mint and cook for 20 minutes until just tender.

Drain well, cool and peel them, then cut into cubes or slices and add dressing as desired.
Serves 6

Hot Potato Salad

675 g/1½ lb waxy potatoes
4 spring onions (scallions), finely chopped
Salt and pepper
4 rashers (slices) streaky bacon, rinds removed, cut into dice
2 tablespoons white wine vinegar
2 tablespoons chopped parsley, to garnish

Boil the potatoes in their skins until just tender. Drain and slice. The skins may be left on or removed, whichever you prefer. Place in a warm bowl and mix in the spring onions. Season with a little salt and plenty of pepper. Meanwhile fry the bacon slowly until crisp. Drain, then add to the salad. Pour the vinegar into the bacon fat, stir and heat through. Pour over the salad and mix gently. Garnish with the parsley.
Serves 6

The Country Salad is a simple and healthy way to bring together a wide range of fresh farm products, including meat, in one stunning dish.

Country Salad

In the French or Italian countryside, spicy additions can turn the humble potato salad into a meal in itself. If you can't find the waxy variety, small new potatoes boiled in their skins and peeled will do for this recipe.

675 g/1½ lb potatoes
2 red peppers (capsicums, bell peppers), cut into rings
200 g/7 oz cooked pork sausage, sliced
2 shallots, very finely sliced
4 firm tomatoes, quartered
175 ml/6 fl oz/¾ cup vinaigrette dressing, (p.13)
2 hard-boiled eggs, chopped and sieved (strained), to garnish
100 g/3½ oz black olives, to garnish

Boil the potatoes (p. 10), slice into thick rounds and place them into a large dish. Add the peppers, sausage, shallots and tomatoes. Pour the vinaigrette over and gently mix through the salad. Garnish with the eggs and olives.
Serves 6

Sweet Potato and Coconut Pudding

Because of its relative sweetness, sweet potato is used much more widely in desserts than is ordinary potato. Coming from the Pacific, its flavour blends well with coconut to provide unusual and tasty puddings.

900 g/2 lb sweet potatoes
Peel and juice of 2 limes or lemons
2 egg yolks
175 g/6 oz/1 cup soft brown sugar
185 g/6 oz/2 cups desiccated (shredded) coconut
½ teaspoon ground cinnamon
3 drops of vanilla essence (extract)

Peel the potatoes, cut into even-sized chunks and boil together with the peel of 1 lime until tender. Drain and mash the potatoes. Allow to cool.

Beat together the egg yolks and sugar. Add to the potatoes and mix in the remaining ingredients, including the peel and juice. Butter a heatproof dish and pour in the mixture. Put in a preheated oven at 180°C/350°F/gas 4 and bake for 1 hour until the pudding has risen and the top is golden brown.

Serves 6

When preparing Sweet Potato and Coconut Pudding, choose the orange-pink variety of vegetable to add greater colour to the dish.

Steaming can be used as an alternative to boiling, and recipes are therefore interchangeable. It is better to use only waxy potatoes when steaming. Place the peeled or unpeeled vegetable directly in a steamer basket in a pan containing 5 cm/2 inches of boiling water, making sure the water does not touch the bottom of the basket. Cover the pan and steam the potatoes for 20–30 minutes until tender. You may have to add a little more boiling water at some time through the cooking process.

When the potatoes are to be used in a salad, refresh them under cold water, or cover with a cloth if they are to be kept warm.

Lots of delicious variations can be used to make your steamed potato dishes extra special. Try adding aromatic seasonings to the boiling water. The steam will impart a subtle flavour to the potatoes. Garlic, fresh root ginger, fresh or dried herbs, cinnamon sticks, peppercorns, juniper berries or even wine are just some of the things you can experiment with.

Different Types of Steamers

Multi-tiered metal steamer over base saucepan of boiling water.

Thai basket steamer which will fit over most saucepans.

Chinese bamboo steamers that stack to steam several types of food simultaneously.

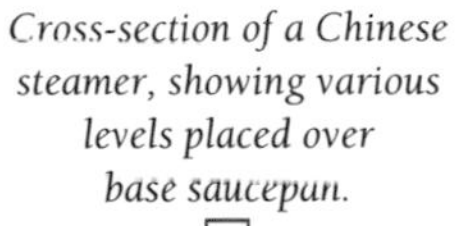
Cross-section of a Chinese steamer, showing various levels placed over base saucepan.

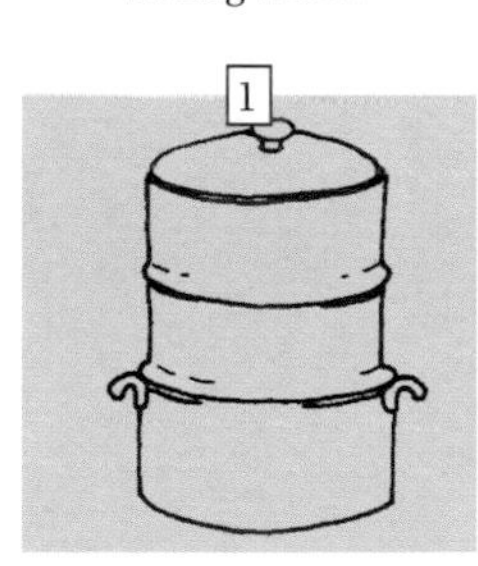

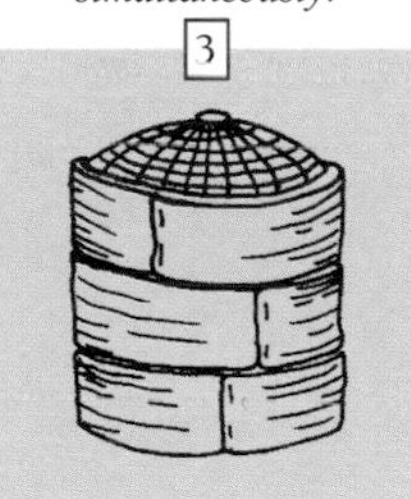

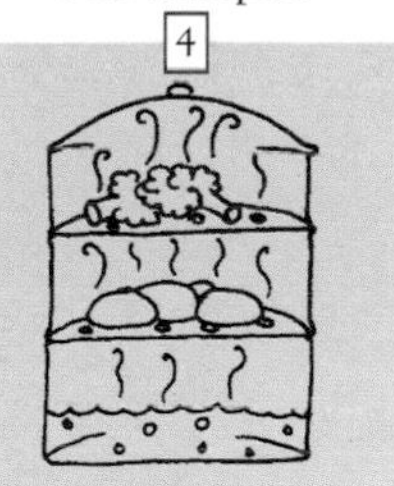

Caramelized Potatoes

These potatoes work well with roast lamb or turkey. Sweet-tooths will love them.

16 small new or waxy potatoes
15 g/6 oz/¾ cup caster (superfine) sugar
1 tablespoon melted butter
1 tablespoon sunflower oil
Pepper

Steam the potatoes until tender. Place the sugar in a large, heavy frying pan (skillet) over a low–medium heat and cook, stirring frequently, with a wooden spoon. After 5 minutes the sugar will melt and start to boil. Continue to boil, without stirring, for another 3 minutes or until it turns golden brown and is still syrupy. Working quickly, add the melted butter and oil and stir until well blended. Add the cooked potatoes, shaking the pan continuously until the potatoes are evenly coated with the caramel. Season with pepper and serve at once.
Serves 4

Greek-Style Potato Salad

A refreshing salad to have on a hot day. Turn it into a colourful occasion by mixing red with green or yellow peppers.

900 g/2 lb small new potatoes, unpeeled
125 ml/4 fl oz/½ cup lemon juice
125 ml/4 fl oz/½ cup olive oil
2 garlic cloves, crushed
1½ tablespoons chopped mint
1 tablespoon chopped oregano
Salt and pepper
1 red onion, thinly sliced
2 peppers (capsicums, bell peppers), cut into rings
175 g/6 oz feta cheese, crumbled
2 tomatoes, cut into small segments
90 g/3 oz/⅔ cup black olives, stoned (pitted)
6 anchovy fillets if liked, to garnish

Steam the potatoes for 10 minutes until tender (p. 17). Allow to cool slightly. Whisk together the lemon juice, oil, garlic, mint and oregano until well blended and season with salt and pepper.

Place the potatoes (cut them into halves if they are too big) into a serving bowl, add half the dressing, toss together, then leave to cool completely. The potatoes will take up more of the dressing if slightly warm.

When cool, add the onion, peppers, cheese, tomatoes and olives, and pour over the remaining dressing. Garnish with the anchovies and serve at room temperature or chilled.
Serves 6

Making Potato Scones

Use a large mixing bowl to combine the dry ingredients.

1

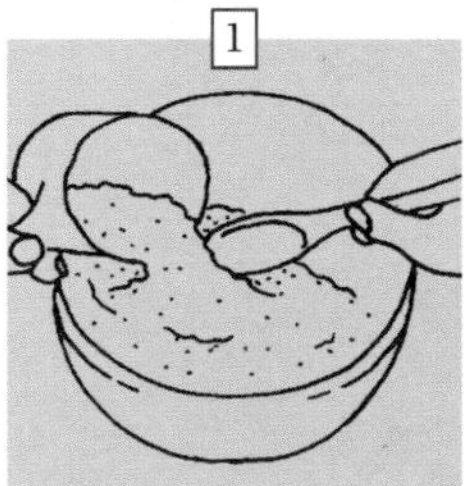

Use fingertips to rub the flour mixture to a bread-crumb-like consistency.

2

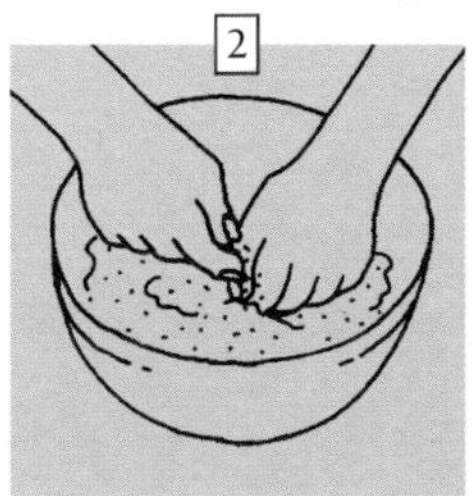

Stir in the egg, herbs, spices, liquid ingredients and diced potatoes.

3

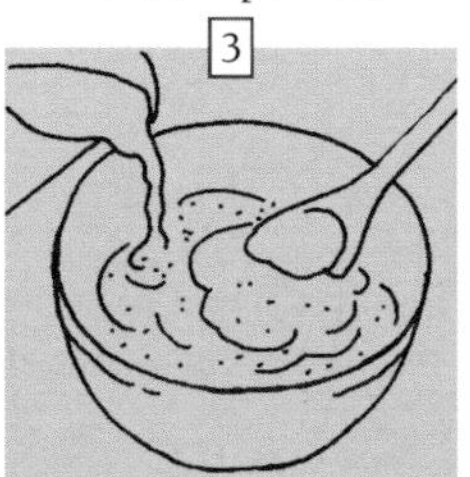

Drop spoonfuls of potato dough onto a baking tray.

4

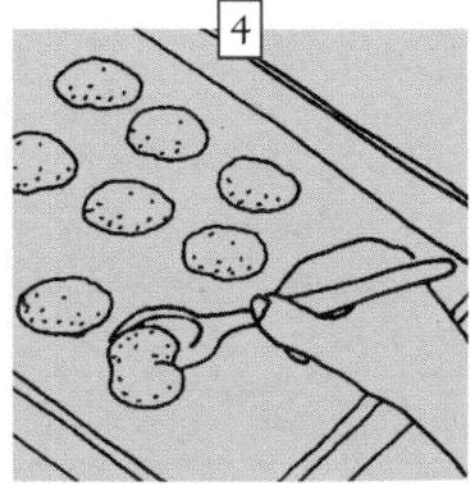

Microwaving. *Not everybody is happy using a microwave oven, but it has one distinct advantage—instantaneous heat control. This is very important where you want to preserve the colour of the vegetable flesh. Microwave radiation also cooks much faster than conventional baking or roasting techniques, as it has the ability to penetrate the potato to its centre or thickest part. It is also a great energy saver, concentrating heat on the food and not the surroundings as happens in a normal gas or electric oven.*

One of the greatest drawbacks is that it does not produce the browning effect that baking or roasting does or therefore the associated flavours that emerge with these processes. Nevertheless, microwaving can be a nutritious way to cook, especially if cooking whole potatoes in their jackets.

Choose uniformly sized vegetables and prick the skin to allow the build-up of steam inside the potato to escape. Cook on high for about 2 minutes, (microwave wattage differs according to brand, so be guided by the model's instruction booklet), then leave to stand for 2 minutes before eating. If you want a quick oven-steamed potato, half-cook in the microwave on high, then transfer to a preheated oven at 200°C/400°F/gas 6 for a further 10 minutes.

Potatoes that have been peeled and sliced can also be cooked in a microwave. Place in a microwave-proof dish, add a tablespoon of water, cover with cling film (plastic wrap) which has been pierced with one or two small holes, and cook on high for 5 minutes or until the vegetable is tender. Leave to stand for 4 minutes. Depending on the type of potato used, this is an ideal way to prepare potatoes for salad.

Sweet Potato Pancakes

Choose the orange-fleshed sweet potato for this dish. It can be served for breakfast with honey and butter or as a dessert with honey and sweetened cream.

4 large eggs
½ teaspoon salt
½ teaspoon baking powder
2 tablespoons flour
1 tablespoon caster (superfine) sugar
250 g/9 oz/1¾ cups mashed cooked sweet potato
2½ tablespoons melted butter
4 tablespoons milk
¼ teaspoon ground cinnamon
Freshly grated nutmeg
1 teaspoon grated ginger
2 tablespoons sunflower oil

Beat together all the ingredients except the oil until smooth. Heat a non-stick frying pan (skillet) or griddle until very hot. Coat the frying pan lightly with oil. Drop tablespoons of batter into the pan and rotate so that the batter spreads and forms nicely rounded circles. Cook for 3–4 minutes until bubbles appear on top. Flip over and cook the other side for 1 minute. Repeat until all the batter has been used, re-coating the pan with oil as you go. Keep the pancakes warm in the oven at 120°C/250°F/gas ½ until ready to serve.

Serves 4

Above: Chunky potato cubes spread throughout the floury dough add an unusual texture and appearance to this scone mixture. Right: Potato Scones with the added flavours of caraway, garlic and cheese need only a light cottage cheese as a side-serving. Try serving with soup instead of crusty bread.

Potato Scones

The ingredients may look formidable but the preparation and cooking are relatively simple and the results delicious.

300 g/11 oz firm waxy potatoes
150 g/5 oz/1¼ cups flour
30 g/1 oz/¼ cup grated Parmesan cheese
2 teaspoons baking powder
1 teaspoon dry mustard
½ teaspoon salt
¼ teaspoon pepper
60 g/2 oz/¼ cup butter, cut into dice and chilled
2 tablespoons olive oil
1 large egg, lightly beaten
2 garlic cloves, crushed
1 tablespoon caraway seeds
75 ml/2½ fl oz/4 tablespoons skimmed milk
Low-fat soft cheese

Steam the potatoes until tender (p. 17). Peel, dice into 6 mm/¼ inch pieces and set to one side.

Combine the flour, Parmesan cheese, baking powder, mustard, salt and pepper. With the fingertips, rub the cold butter into the flour mixture until it resembles course breadcrumbs. Stir in the oil, egg, garlic, caraway seeds and milk until just combined. Gently fold in the diced potatoes and distribute them throughout the floury mixture. Try not to 'mash' the potatoes.

Drop round tablespoonfuls of the mixture on to an ungreased baking sheet about 2.5 cm/1 inch apart. Bake in a preheated oven at 200°C/400°F/gas 6 for 12–15 minutes or until the edges of the scones are slightly golden. Serve with soft cheese or as an accompaniment to soup.
Makes 12

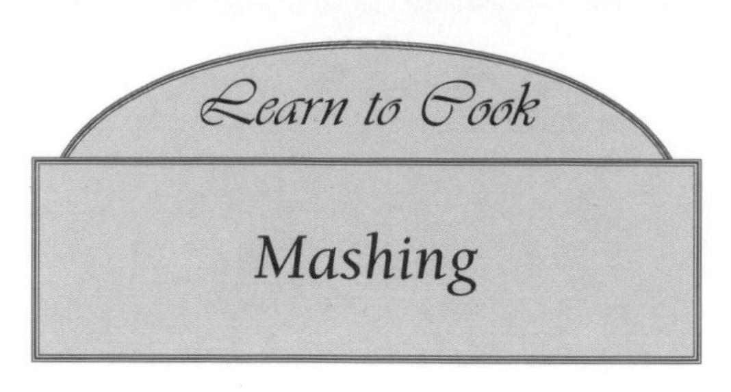

Mashing

This is strictly not a cooking method at all, but every self-respecting book about potatoes needs to give the mashing preparation a special mention. The mashed potato is not required to hold its original shape, therefore floury or mealy potatoes high in starch are the best varieties to use. Experienced cooks avoid food processors and opt instead for the old-fashioned potato masher or a large fork.

The potatoes are first cooked by boiling (p. 10) or steaming (p. 17). It is better to cook the potatoes in their skins to prevent them becoming waterlogged. The famous Roux brothers of France recommend putting a quarter of a lemon in the boiling water to prevent the potatoes breaking up.

Peel the potatoes and leave them to stand for about 5 minutes under a clean cloth, then mash while still warm, using an up-and-down motion to incorporate as much air as possible and give the potato a light, fluffy consistency. Additives such as milk and butter are incorporated at this stage.

The consistency of the mash will be determined by its use within the meal you are going to serve. A dryish firm mash will require about 60 g/2 oz/¼ cup butter and 150–175 ml/5–6 fl oz/⅔–¾ cup milk for every 900 g/2 lb potatoes. Warm milk is easier to incorporate than cold. If you must keep the mashed potatoes warm before serving, dot with a couple of teaspoons of butter and cover the dish with foil. Just before serving, whisk the melted butter into the potato.

Mashed Potato

Believe it or not, it takes a very special skill to produce a tantalizing dish of mashed potatoes. They need to be creamy, smooth, light and fluffy all at the same time, and no matter how hard you work at the rest of the menu, someone will always comment on the mashed potato. Use old potatoes with floury flesh.

900 g/2 lb potatoes
45 g/1½ oz/3 tablespoons butter
200 ml/7 fl oz/¾ cup milk, warmed
Salt and pepper, if liked

Place the unpeeled potatoes into a saucepan and just cover with cold water. Bring to the boil, cover the pot and simmer for 25-30 minutes until tender. Drain well, peel and cover with a clean cloth for 5 minutes until all the moisture has evaporated. Wet, soggy potatoes will not beat up into a creamy consistency.

Mash the potatoes with an up-and-down movement, then push to the sides of the pan, creating a well in the middle. Add the milk and butter and, using a fork, incorporate them quickly into the potato until a creamy consistency is reached. Season with salt and pepper.
Serves 4

Quite a few different types of mild-tasting onions are used in the preparation of Mashed Potato and Thyme Soup (p. 27). Mixing lemon thyme with ordinary garden thyme will give a distinctive flavour.

Waxy or floury? *If you are undecided about what sort of potato you have bought, there is a well-known test which will help you decide whether a potato is waxy or floury. Make a solution of 2 parts water to 1 part salt. The waxy potato will float, the floury one will sink.*

Mashed Potatoes

Place unpeeled potatoes in cold water and bring to the boil. Cook.

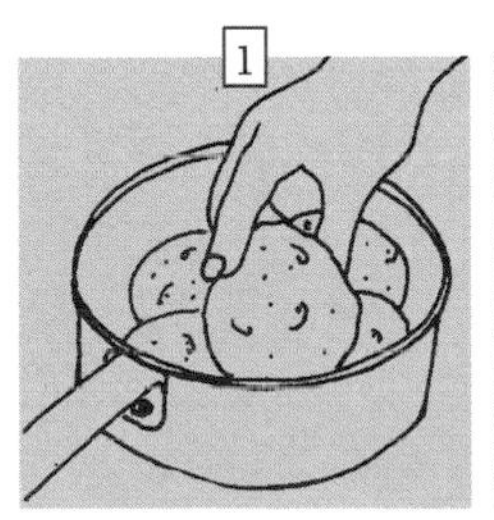

Drain, then peel potatoes and cover with a clean cloth.

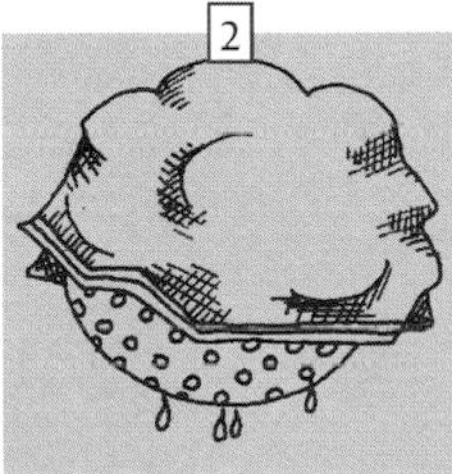

Mash with an up-and-down movement.

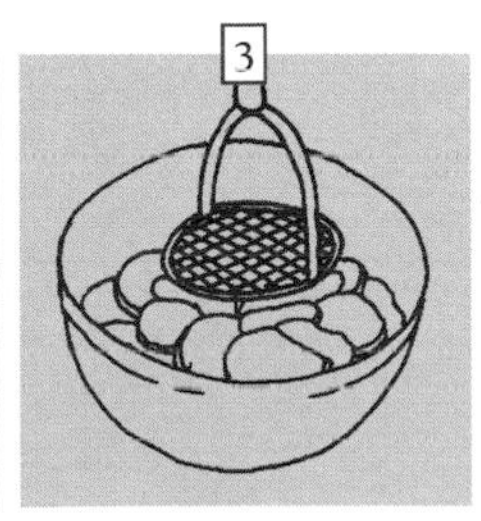

Stir in milk and butter to achieve a creamy consistency.

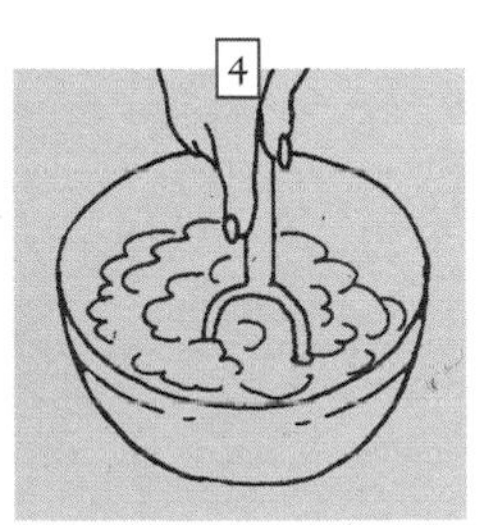

Mashed Potato and Thyme Soup

15 g/½ oz/1 tablespoon butter
1 onion, finely chopped
2 spring onions (scallions), white part only, thinly sliced
3 shallots, very finely chopped
2 teaspoons chopped thyme
450 g/1 lb potatoes, cooked and mashed (p. 22)
4 tablespoons dry white wine
Salt and pepper
3 tablespoons snipped chives, to garnish

Melt the butter in a large heavy-based pan, add the onion, spring onions and shallots and cook for 3–4 minutes until soft but not brown. Stir in the stock and thyme and bring to the boil. Gradually add the mashed potato and bring once again to the boil. Reduce the heat to low, stir in the wine and simmer for 5 minutes. Season with salt and pepper. Serve garnished with chives.
Serves 4

Potato and Onion Soup

This is a classic French soup, easy to prepare, in which you use potatoes of the floury variety because the soup is puréed.

450 g/1 lb potatoes
4 small onions, finely sliced
125 g/4 oz/½ cup butter
60 g/2 oz/½ cup flour
750 ml/1¼ pints/3 cups stock
150 ml/¼ pint/⅔ cup milk
Salt and pepper
1 tablespoon chopped parsley, to garnish

Boil the potatoes in salted water, peel and mash. In a heavy-bottomed 1 litre/1¾ pint/4¼ cups saucepan or casserole dish, sauté the onion in the butter for 5 minutes over a low heat. Add the flour and stir to make a thick paste (roux), then gradually add the hot stock. Bring to the boil and allow to simmer for 5 minutes.

Add the potato, simmer for a further 5 minutes, then add the milk. Season with salt and pepper, then blend in a food processor to liquidize all the ingredients. Garnish with the parsley.
Serves 4

Left: Mashed Potato and Thyme Soup is a thick and creamy with a delightful herby fragrance. Serve with Potato Scones.

Overleaf: Herb and Potato Balls (p. 47) provide a tasty first course. Fresh chives as well as dried herbs are used in this recipe. Deep-fry only a few at a time to preserve their crispness.

Potato and Carrot Casserole

A simple, easy-to-prepare casserole which will no doubt find favour with vegetarian cooks.

675 g/1½ lb old potatoes
60 g/2 oz/4 tablespoons butter
3 tablespoons soured cream
3 tablespoons milk
Salt and pepper
675 g/1½ lb carrots, roughly chopped
1 onion, cut into dice
500 ml/17 fl oz/2¼ cups stock
1 teaspoon French mustard
125 ml/4 fl oz/½ cup mayonnaise
15 g/½ oz/1 tablespoon butter, extra
1 tablespoon milk, extra

Boil the potatoes (p. 10) until tender, drain, cool and peel. Add the butter and mash until smooth. Incorporate the soured cream and milk and season to taste. Place the carrots in a separate saucepan with the onion and stock. Bring to the boil, reduce the heat and simmer for 20 minutes until tender. Drain and reserve 2 tablespoons of the carrot liquid. Transfer the carrot mixture and reserved liquid to a food processor along with the mustard and mayonnaise. Season to taste and purée.

Layer the mashed potato and carrot mixture in a heatproof dish. Brush the top layer with extra milk and dot with the extra butter. Bake in a preheated oven at 180°C/350°F/gas 4 for 30 minutes until the top is golden.

Serves 6

Below and right: Baked Potato and Carrot Casserole is all the vegetable you will need to accompany grilled sausages. An upmarket version of bangers and mash.

Mashed Potatoes with Cream

This one is quite a favourite in Italy.

½ medium onion, sliced
175 g/6 oz/¾ cup butter
1 teaspoon flour
2 teaspoons chopped parsley
Pinch of nutmeg
Salt and pepper
250 ml/8 fl oz/1 cup single (light) cream
900 g/2 lb potatoes, cooked and mashed (p. 22)

Soften the onion in the butter for about 2 minutes over a low heat. Add the flour, parsley, nutmeg, salt and pepper. Heat the mixture through and let it bubble before adding the cream. Stir continuously and bring back to the boil before adding the potatoes. Leave to stand for 5 minutes before serving.
Serves 6

Salting. *Whatever method you are using to cook potatoes, go easy on salt or salty additives. Salt has the effect of drawing out the nutrients from the vegetables and hence destroying the flavour.*

Curried Potato Patties

275 g/10 oz/2 cups hot mashed potato (p. 22)
1 egg
¼ teaspoon curry powder
1 teaspoon chopped parsley
15 g/½ oz/1 tablespoon butter or margarine
1 lemon, cut into wedges

Place the hot mashed potato in a mixing bowl and add the egg, curry powder and parsley. Mix until well blended. On a greased baking sheet, shape the mixture into four patties and flatten slightly in the centres. Put a dot of butter in the centre of each patty and bake in a preheated oven at 200°C/400°F/gas 6 for 10 minutes until heated through. Serve with a squeeze of lemon.
Serves 4

Discoloration. *The unattractive darkening of potatoes which sometimes happens after peeling can be eliminated by adding a little lemon juice or vinegar to the cooking water. This discoloration is not harmful. If black spots appear during boiling, add ½ teaspoon cream of tartar for every 450 ml/¾ pint/2 cups of cooking water after the potatoes are half done.*

Chocolate Potato Cake

A great treat when served with potato cream!

125 g/4 oz/½ cup butter
125 g/4 oz/½ cup sugar
225 g/8 oz/1¾ cups mashed potato (p. 22)
155 g/5 oz/1¼ cups flour
Pinch of salt
2 teaspoons baking powder
2 tablespoons cocoa
A few drops of vanilla essence (extract)

Beat together the butter and sugar and mix in the potato. Sift in the flour, salt, baking powder and cocoa. Add the vanilla essence and enough water to make a stiff paste. Pour the mixture into a buttered and floured cake tin and bake in a preheated oven at 190°C/375°F/gas 5 for 2 hours. Allow to shrink and cool before turning out. Set aside for 24 hours, then slice through the middle, fill and ice on top with potato cream.
Serves 8

Potato Cream

An unusual filling or topping for cakes. Vanilla sugar is made by placing 1-2 vanilla pods (beans) in an airtight container of sugar–for this recipe, caster (superfine) sugar is best–to absorb the distinctive taste and aroma.

225 g/8 oz/1¾ cups mashed potato (p. 22)
275 g/10 oz/1¼ cups caster (superfine) sugar
1 tablespoon vanilla sugar
275 g/10 oz/1¼ cups butter
60 g/2 oz/½ cup walnuts, chopped
2 tablespoons rum, flambéed

Press the potatoes through a sieve (strainer) twice to make them extra smooth, then mix in the sugars. Cream the butter, add to the potatoes and whisk until light and fluffy. Stir in the walnuts and rum.

Potato Cream

Press mashed potato twice through a sieve.

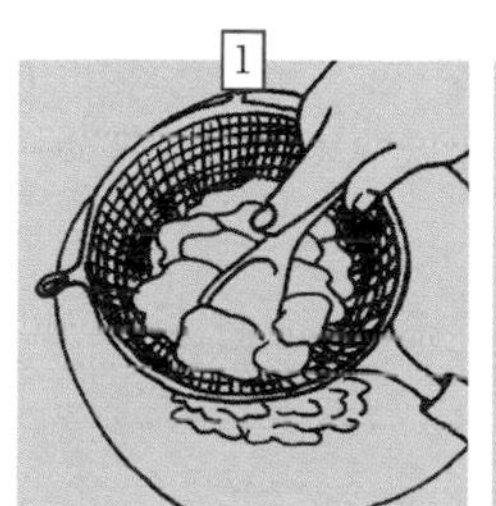

Stir in sugars, cream and butter, then whisk until light and fluffy.

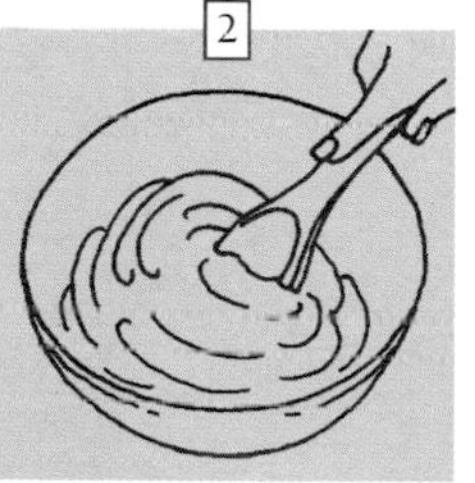

Add walnuts to the mixture.

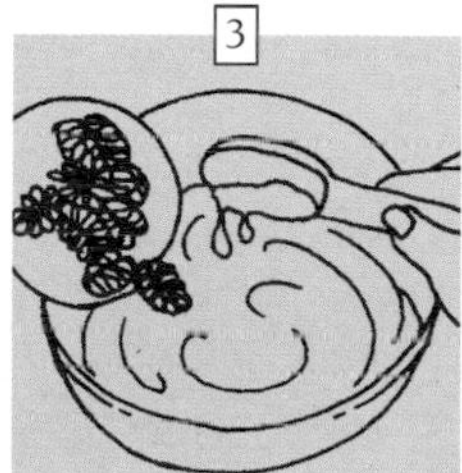

Stir rum slowly into potato cream and stir.

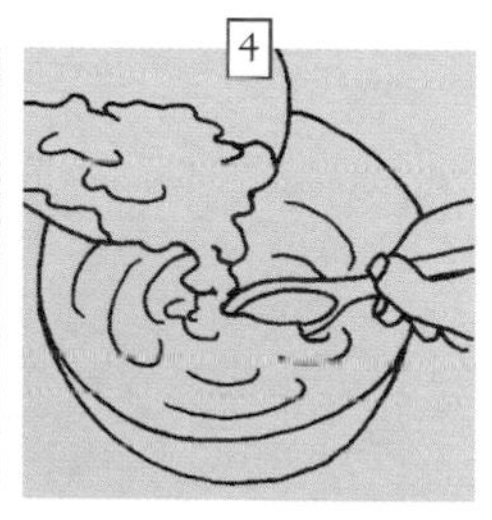

This technique involves completely surrounding the food with a hot enclosure, namely an oven, and the cooking relies on radiated heat from the walls or hot-air convection currents. Temperatures range from 150°C/300°F/gas 2 to 240°C/475°F/gas 9.

Potatoes that are floury or mealy in texture are best suited to baking because the starches expand under the intense heat and the potatoes become fluffy on the inside.

Place the potatoes directly on to the oven rack and bake in a preheated oven at 230°C/450°F/gas 8 for 1 hour. Do not place the potatoes too close to one another as this reduces the crispness of the skin. If you like very crisp skins and fluffy centres, bake for over 1 hour. Potatoes can also be wrapped in foil before baking, but the result will be a soggy potato with a mushy texture.

Yoghurt and fresh chives make a nutritious filling for Crunchy Baked Potato Skins (p. 36). Vary the flavour by adding different herbs or spices to the yoghurt.

Baked Stuffed Potato

Large floury potatoes are ideal for this rather filling starter.

6 large potatoes
3 spring onions (scallions)
60 g/2 oz/¼ cup butter
125 ml/4 fl oz/½ cup soured cream
2 egg yolks
Salt and pepper
1 teaspoon paprika

Place the potatoes directly on to the oven rack and bake in a preheated oven at 200°C/400°F/gas 6 for 30–60 minutes until tender.

Meanwhile remove about 2 cm/¾ inch of green from the spring onions and cut into thin round slices (save the white tops for another use). Melt the butter in a small pan and sauté the spring onions until tender, then set aside. Beat together the soured cream and egg yolks. When the potatoes are baked, remove from the oven (but do not turn off), cut lengthwise into halves and scoop out the flesh without damaging the shells. Mash the flesh and incorporate the spring onions and melted butter, then beat in the soured cream and egg yolks. Season with salt and pepper.

Fill the potato shells with the mixture, heaping it towards the centre, and sprinkle with paprika. Return the shells to the oven and bake for a further 10 minutes until golden brown on top.
Serves 6

Baked Potatoes Italian Style

A few extra additions to the basic baked potato makes a very tasty appetizer.

2 large floury potatoes
1 large tomato
8 black olives, stoned (pitted) and cut into dice
30 g/1 oz/2 tablespoons margarine
1 teaspoon chopped basil
Pepper
75 g/2½ oz/½ cup mozzarella cheese, thinly sliced
4 anchovy fillets, drained and patted dry

Bake the potatoes as in the previous recipe. Drop the tomato into boiling water for 2 minutes, peel off the skin and cut the flesh into dice. Halve the potatoes horizontally and scoop out the flesh. Mash well and beat in the tomato, olives, margarine, basil and pepper to taste.

Fill the potato shells with the mixture, lay the cheese over the top and arrange the anchovy fillets diagonally across the cheese. Place the potatoes onto a baking sheet and return to the oven for a further 15 minutes until the cheese has melted.
Serves 4

Sweet Potato Purée

This is a good accompaniment to strong, meaty dishes.

900 g/2 lb sweet potatoes
2 large white floury potatoes
Salt and pepper
90 g/3 oz/⅓ cup salted butter

Bake all the potatoes in a preheated oven at 200°C/400°F/gas 6 for 1 hour until the flesh is soft. Cut in half and scoop out the flesh. Mash and warm through in a saucepan. Season with salt and pepper, then briskly whisk in the butter. Serve with an extra knob of butter.
Serves 6

Oven-Baked Potato Chips (French Fries)

If you don't feel confident with the deep-frying method, try making chips in the oven. The small quantity of oil used provides a satisfying alternative to the deep-fried version.

675 g/1½ lb large potatoes
1 teaspoon chilli or curry powder, if liked
2 teaspoons sunflower oil
¼ teaspoon salt

Peel and cut the potatoes lengthwise into slices about 12 mm/½ inch thick. Cut each slice lengthwise into 12 mm/½ inch strips and place in a large bowl. Toss with the chilli powder if using and sprinkle on the oil. Toss so that the potatoes are well coated.

Arrange the strips on a large preheated baking sheet and cook in a preheated oven at 240°C/475°F/gas 9 for 20 minutes. Turn the chips over and bake for a further 20 minutes or until crisp and browned. Sprinkle with salt and serve hot.
Serves 4

French Fries

Cut potato into 12 mm/½ inch slices.

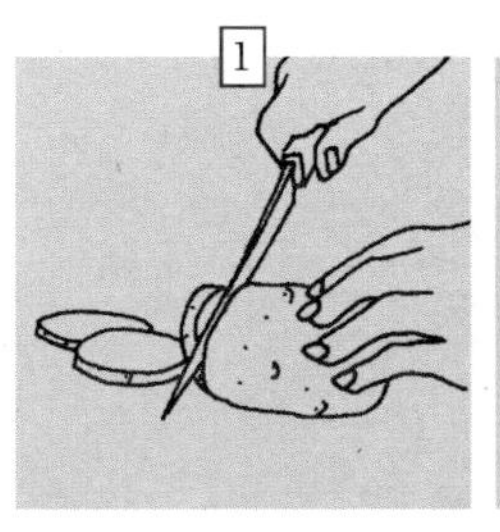

Cut each slice into 12 mm/½ inch strips.

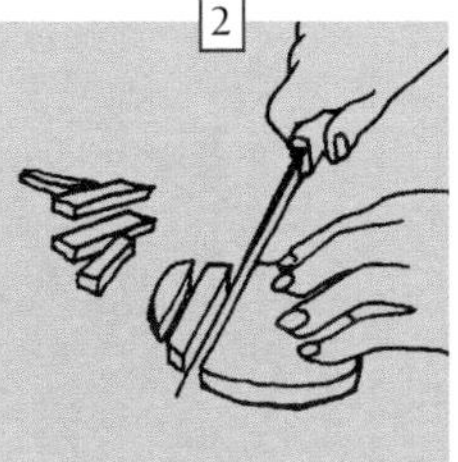

Dredge fries with chilli powder and sprinkle with oil.

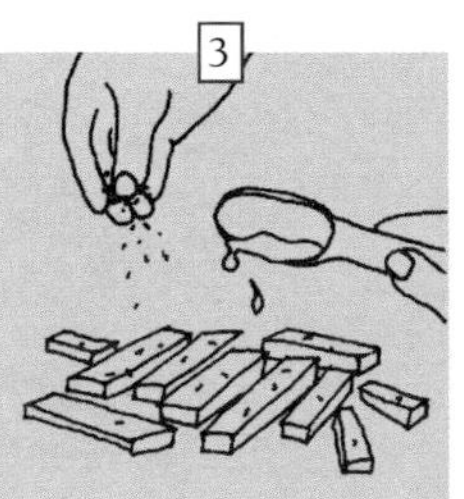

Arrange potato strips on a hot baking sheet.

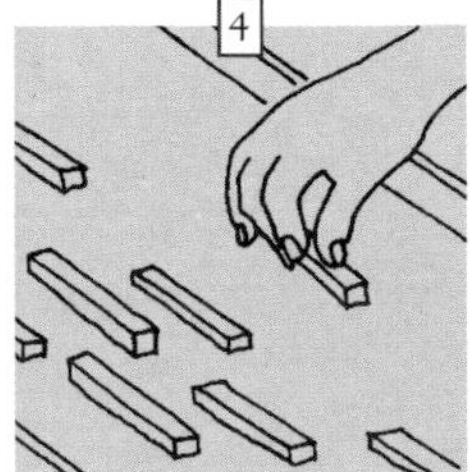

Gruyère Potatoes

This is a variation of a famous French potato dish called gratin dauphinois. It may sound complicated but is really quite easy. You can substitute single (light) cream for the milk (or use a mixture of both) and add a little thinly sliced onion and crushed garlic if liked. The beauty of this dish is that it can be prepared ahead.

900 g/2 lb potatoes
125 g/4 oz/1 cup grated Gruyère cheese
Salt and pepper
Freshly grated nutmeg
550 ml/18 fl oz/2¼ cups milk
30 g/1 oz/2 tablespoons butter

Peel the potatoes and slice thinly but do not soak in cold water. Lightly grease a 1.25 litre/2¼ pint/5¾ cup shallow heatproof dish and layer the potatoes and most of the cheese into the dish. Season and sprinkle with nutmeg. Top with the remaining cheese and pour over the milk, which should just cover the potatoes. Dot the surface with the butter, cover with foil and bake in a preheated oven at 180°C/350°F/gas 4 for 1½ hours. The potatoes should be quite tender and most of the liquid absorbed.

If not served immediately, cool and chill in the refrigerator until required. To serve, uncover and bake in a preheated oven at 180°C/350°F/gas 4 for 45 minutes until the top is golden brown.
Serves 6

Storing. *Prolonged storage after buying will reduce the vitamin C content of your potato. The same thing happens if you keep a peeled potato in cold water for any length of time.Store in a dark, cool, airy place such as a cellar or a cupboard with air holes. Old potatoes are most amenable to long storage. New potatoes should be eaten as soon as possible.*

Baked Potatoes, French Style

900 g/2 lb potatoes, peeled
2 tablespoons French mustard
2 tablespoons snipped chives
300 ml/½ pint/1¼ cups milk
Salt and pepper
2 tablespoons melted butter

Cut the potatoes into 12 mm/½ inch slices and arrange a single layer in a greased 1 litre/1¾ pint/4¼ cup heatproof dish. Combine the mustard, chives, milk and seasoning and pour a little over the layer of potatoes. Repeat this process until all the ingredients have been used up. Brush the top layer with the melted butter, and cover the dish with foil. Bake in a preheated oven at 180°C/350°F/gas 4 for 1¾–2 hours until the potatoes are tender and can be pierced with a fork.
Serves 6

Crunchy Baked Potato Skins

So much store is placed on the nutritional value of the potato skin, American cooks have come up with a novel way to serve the skin as a quick and easy snack or a starter before the main course.

4 floury potatoes
4 tablespoons sunflower oil
Salt and pepper
300 ml/½ pint/1¼ cups plain yoghurt
2 tablespoons snipped chives

Pierce the potatoes liberally with a skewer, place them directly on to the oven rack and bake in a preheated oven at 200°C/400°F/gas 6 for 1 hour until tender. Cut each potato lengthwise and scoop out most of the flesh, taking care not to split the skins.

Lightly oil a baking sheet. Stand the skins on the sheet and brush the potatoes inside and out with the oil. Sprinkle with plenty of salt and pepper. Increase the oven temperature to 220°C/425°F/gas 7 and bake for 10 minutes until crisp.

Meanwhile, whisk the yoghurt and chives together and spoon into a small bowl. Serve the potato skins while quite hot with the yoghurt dressing on the side.

Serves 4

Irish Stew

An old tried and true but much-loved recipe which comes to life with quality cuts of meat.

450 g/1 lb lamb fillets, cut into cubes
900 g/2 lb potatoes, sliced
2 large onions, sliced
Salt and pepper
2 tablespoons chopped parsley, to garnish

Line a casserole dish with alternate layers of lamb, potato and onion, seasoning with salt and pepper as you go. Finish with a layer of potatoes, which should completely cover the top of the casserole. Pour in sufficient water to cover the casserole halfway. Cover and bake in a preheated oven at 190°C/375°F/gas 5 for 3 hours. Serve sprinkled with parsley.

Serves 4

Baked potatoes are a very healthy way to eat compared to boiling potatoes because there is no loss of goodness or flavour into the water that is later thrown away.

Crunchy Baked Potato Skins make an ideal starter to a main meal. The hot crispy skin balances the cold creamy filling.

Floury varieties are the best potatoes for roasting. This method works very well with small, unpeeled new potatoes or larger varieties that can be quartered or cut into large cubes. The potatoes are ready when the thickest part can be pierced with a fork. Delicious variations can be achieved by adding fresh or dried herbs such as rosemary, or roasting with onions and a sprinkling of paprika.

Unpeeled Roast Potatoes

900 g/2 lb small or medium old potatoes
2 tablespoons olive or sunflower oil
2 tablespoons chopped rosemary, if liked

Cut the potatoes into 2.5 cm/1 inch cubes. Pour the oil into a large shallow roasting pan and place in a preheated oven at 220°C/425°F/gas 7 until it becomes quite hot. Add the potatoes to the oil and stir so that they are well coated. Roast in the oven for 1 hour, stirring occasionally, until crisp and golden brown. The rosemary may be added during one of the stirring periods.
Serves 4

Crispy Little Roast Potatoes

An appetizing dish of small, crispy roast potatoes, highly seasoned, to serve with drinks before dinner. You can use any variety of potato for this dish. While the cooking technique is simple, set aside a leisurely 3 hours for preparation time.

1.5 kg/3¼ lb potatoes
175 g/6 oz/½ cup flour
Salt and pepper
250 ml/8 fl oz/1 cup olive or sunflower oil

Parboil the potatoes in their skins for 15 minutes, drain, cool, then peel. Cut into small, even-sized pieces and roll in the flour which has been seasoned with salt and pepper. Divide the oil between 2 roasting pans no more than 5 mm/¼ inch deep, and place the pans in a preheated oven at 200°C/400°F/gas 6 until hot. Place the potatoes in the hot oil and roast in the oven for at least 2 hours until very crispy. Season with salt and pepper and serve.
Serves 8 as an appetizer

The decorative shape of roasted Hasselbach Potatoes (p. 40), with tasty inserts of garlic or fresh herbs, offsets plain cuts of roast meat.

During the preparation of Hasselbach potatoes, separate the incisions with fresh garlic, oregano or any other fresh herb of your choice.

Hasselbach Potatoes

Very easy to prepare and a novelty to look at. If you want to enliven the dish, add crushed garlic juice and chopped oregano to the oil. It goes well with any meat or fish dish.

16 small baking potatoes
3 tablespoons oil
Salt and pepper

Peel and cut the potatoes across their width at 6 mm/¼ inch intervals but only three-quarters of the way through. Place in a single layer in an oiled roasting pan. Brush with the oil and season. Roast, uncovered, in a preheated oven at 180°C/350°F/gas 4 for 1 hour or until cooked through.
Serves 8

Hasselbach Potatoes

Cut the potato across its width but only ¾ of the way through.

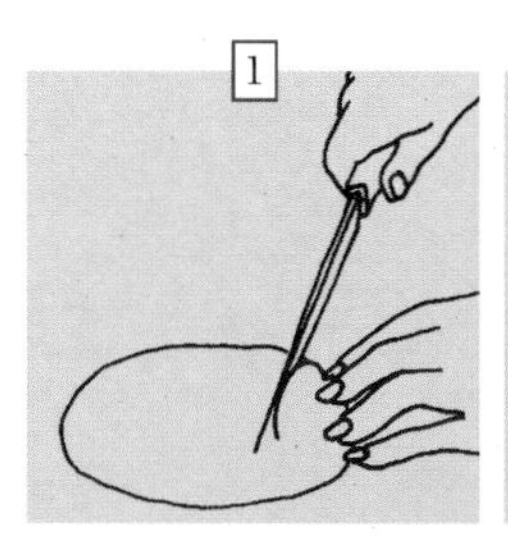

Continue slicing the potato along its length at 6 mm/¼ inch intervals.

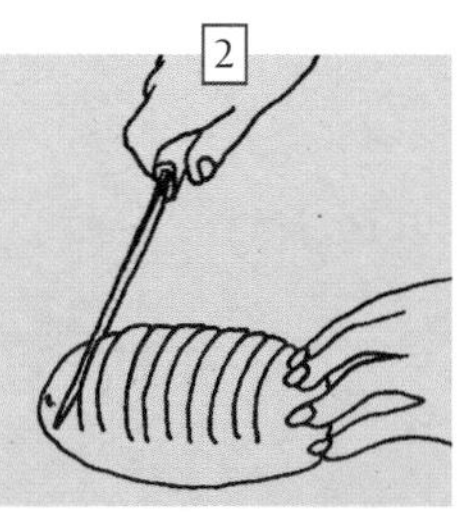

Place potatoes in a single layer in an oiled roasting pan.

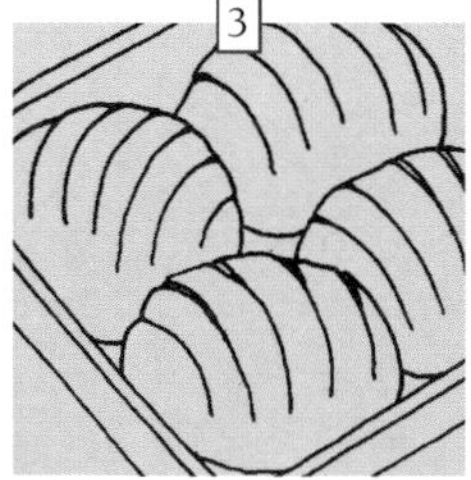

Brush the surface of each potato with oil and bake.

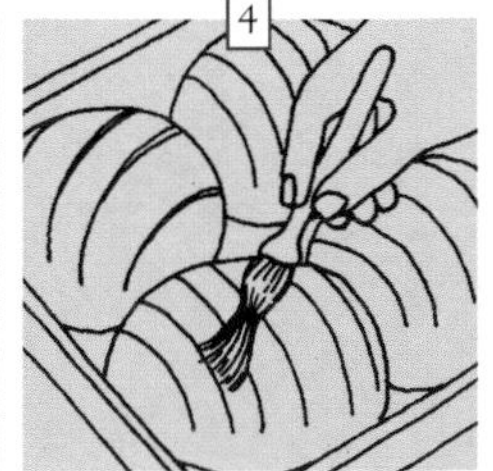

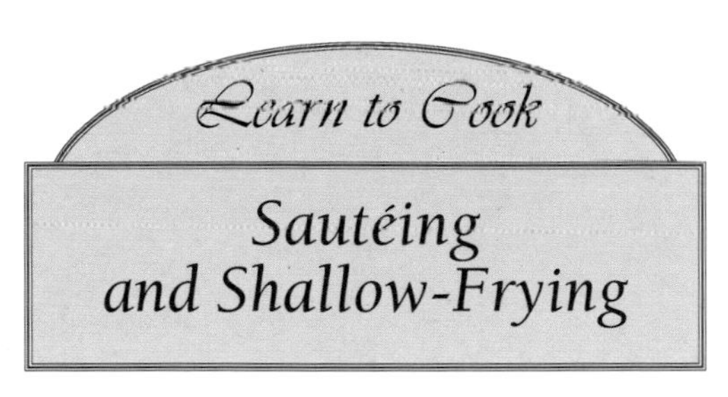

Sautéing and Shallow-Frying

Sauté means to cook or lightly fry food rapidly in small amounts of oil or fat, turning or stirring frequently. The idea is to have only a very thin layer of oil between the pan and the food. This has a threefold effect. It lubricates the food, preventing sticking; it brings the food into more even contact with the heat source; and, depending on the type of oil or fat used, it flavours the food.

Firm-fleshed potatoes are the ones best suited to sautéing. The type of oil or fat is also important. If using butter, always use unsalted as salt will only lead to burning in the pan. Mixing 2–4 tablespoons of oil to every 60 g/2 oz/¼ cup butter will solve this problem. Another alternative is to use only clarified butter (ghee), which can be purchased from most supermarkets. Suitable fats include beef, lard (pork) and bacon fat, and suitable oils include olive, peanut (groundnut) or corn for flavour, or sunflower, which stands up to high temperatures. Remember always to heat the pan first, then add the cold oil, and always use a wide, shallow, heavy frying pan (skillet).

Sautéed Lemon Potatoes

900 g/2 lb firm waxy potatoes
15 g/6 oz/¾ cup clarified butter (ghee)
Salt and pepper
Juice of 2 lemons
1 tablespoon chopped parsley, to garnish

Boil the potatoes in their skins until cooked through. Peel and slice into 6 mm/¼ inch rounds. Melt the butter in a frying pan (skillet), then arrange a layer of potato slices in it. Season and spoon a little of the lemon juice over. Repeat the process until all the potatoes are used. Pour any remaining lemon juice into the pan and cook, covered, over a low heat for 15 minutes. Remove the lid and cook for a further 10 minutes. The top layer of potatoes will be saturated with butter and juice while the bottom layer will have formed a crisp crust. Remove from the pan and garnish with parsley.
Serves 6

Crispy chips. *Soaking cut potatoes in salty water helps make chips extra crispy. Always pat them dry in a tea-towel (dishcloth) before plunging into the hot oil.*

Veal with Potatoes

An aromatic dish of Mediterranean origin.

675 g/1½ lb waxy potatoes
220 g/7 oz/1 cup clarified butter (ghee)
900 g/2 lb veal cutlets
2 onions, sliced
450 g/1 lb ripe tomatoes, peeled and chopped
125 ml/4 fl oz/½ cup dry white wine
600 ml/1 pint/2½ cups chicken stock
4 bay leaves
Salt and white pepper

Peel the potatoes and slice in half horizontally. Heat a large frying pan (skillet) and melt half the butter. Sauté the potatoes until half-cooked. Set aside, then fry the cutlets for a couple of minutes on each side.

Pile the potatoes on one side of a large casserole dish and the meat on the other. In another pan, melt the remaining butter and sauté the onions until they begin to wilt. Add the tomatoes. Simmer for a few minutes, then add the wine, stock and bay leaves. Cook for a further 5 minutes, then pour over the meat and potatoes. Season, cover with foil, then place the lid on top to seal firmly. Bake in a preheated oven at 160°C/325°F/gas 3 for 2 hours.
Serves 6

Spiced Potatoes

A taste of the exotic East with spices and herbs to sharpen the flavour of new potatoes.

900 g/2 lb small new potatoes
60 g/2 oz/¼ cup clarified butter (ghee)
2 teaspoons turmeric
4 teaspoons ground coriander
4 teaspoons cumin seeds
2 garlic cloves, crushed
4 teaspoons sugar
Salt and pepper
1 tablespoon chopped parsley, to garnish
1 tablespoon snipped chives, to garnish

Parboil the potatoes for 5 minutes, then drain. Melt the butter in a heatproof dish and when bubbling add the spices and garlic and sauté for 1 minute. Add the potatoes and stir until they are well coated. Sprinkle the sugar over and season. Cook in a preheated oven at 180°C/350°F/gas 4 for 30 minutes, turning occasionally. Serve garnished with the parsley and chives.
Serves 6

Veal with Potato is a hearty dish with all the flavours and aromas of the Mediterranean.

Hashed Brown Potatoes

Place the potatoes in cold water, bring to the boil and cook.

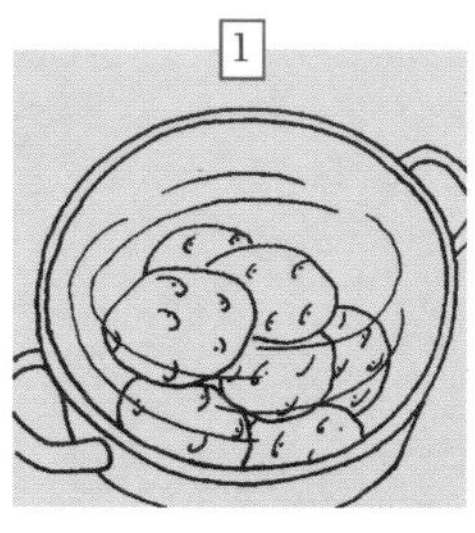

Peel and dice the boiled potatoes.

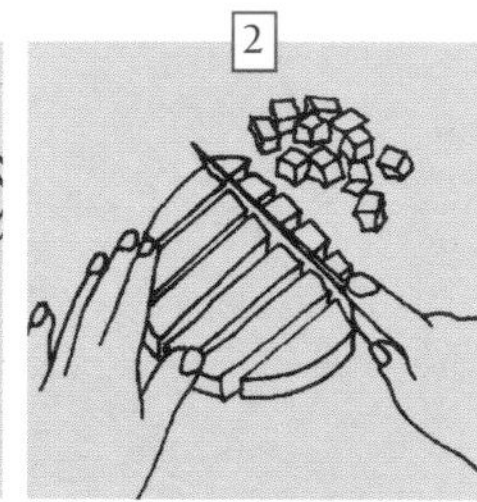

Press the diced potatoes into small pancake-shaped masses.

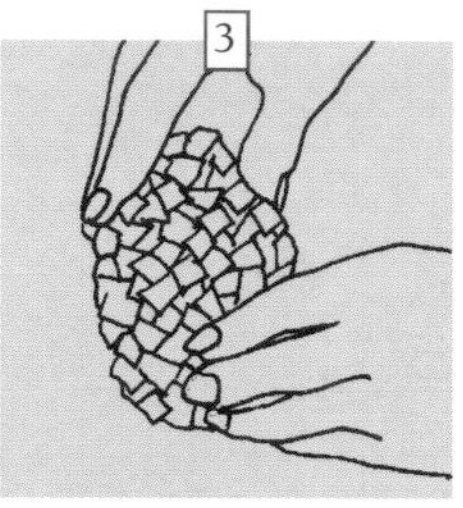

Sauté on both sides until brown and crusty.

Hashed Brown Potatoes

900 g/2 lb potatoes, unpeeled
90 g/3 oz/½ cup bacon fat
Salt and pepper
6 tablespoons chopped spring onion (scallion) tops, to garnish
3 tablespoons chopped parsley, to garnish

Cover the potatoes with cold water and bring to the boil, then simmer for 20 minutes until tender. Drain, cool, then refrigerate without peeling. This step may be done the day before so you can get on with the cooking at breakfast the next day.

Heat a thin film of the fat in a frying pan (skillet) no deeper than 6 mm/¼ inch. Peel and dice the potatoes, add them to the pan, press them into a mass with a spatula, and cook until brown and crusty. Turn the potatoes over and season the browned side with salt and pepper. Do not be alarmed if the potato breaks up or crumbles—this only adds to the texture of the dish. Continue to sauté until the second side is brown and crusty. Flip once more, seasoning again with salt and pepper. To serve, cut into wedges and sprinkle with the spring onion tops and parsley.
Serves 6

The first stage of sautéing potatoes with the potatoes half cooked and glistening with butter.

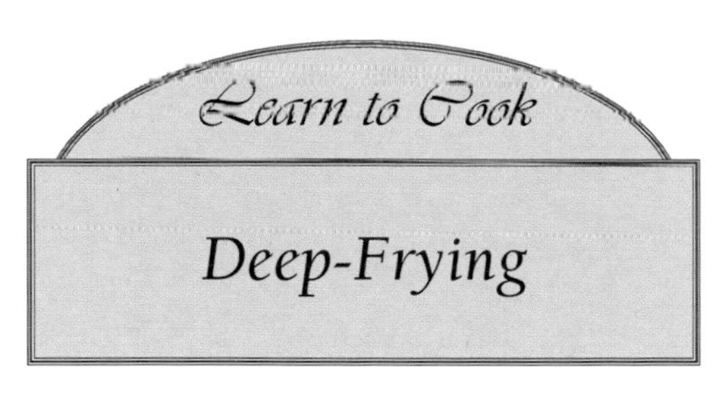

Deep-frying differs from sautéing in that enough oil is used to immerse the food completely. In this way it resembles boiling, except that the temperature of the oil or fat is at least twice that of water, and food will not only cook more quickly but brown on the outside as well. A pan that is deeper than it is wide is the best cooking utensil to use.

It is also wise not to crowd the pan, so cook your potatoes (which have been cut into uniform pieces for even cooking) in small batches. When adding oil (remember, cold oil to a warm pan) for deep-frying, add enough to cover the food but don't fill the pan more than half-full. It is always preferable to use fresh oil. Bits of leftover food from previous deep-frying will only cause unpleasant smells and flavours. Mealy or floury potatoes are the best kind for deep-frying. **Caution:** deep-frying is one of the most dangerous of all techniques. Never walk away from the pan of hot oil when deep-frying and always make sure the handle of the pan is turned towards the side of the cooker. If the fat or oil starts to smoke acrid fumes, turn the heat source off immediately and do not attempt to carry the pan anywhere.

Potato Croquettes

This great party-starter involves two techniques: mashing and deep-frying. You can prepare the potato mixtures hours in advance and deep fry at the last moment. Add basil or thyme for a change and use parmesan cheese instead of cheddar cheese.

675 g/1½ lb old potatoes
30 g/1 oz/2 tablespoons butter
1 large onion, cut into dice
45 g/1½ oz/⅓ cup Cheddar cheese
Flour
1 egg
2 tablespoons milk
125 g/4 oz/1 cup packaged dried breadcrumbs
2 tablespoons chopped parsley
Sunflower oil for deep-frying

Cover the potatoes with cold water, bring to the boil, cover and simmer for 30 minutes until tender. Drain, peel and mash. Melt the butter in a pan and cook the onion until transparent. Add to the mashed potatoes and mix well. Cut the cheese into 6 mm x 4 cm/¼ x 1½ inch strips. Mould 2 tablespoons of potato mixture around the cheese strips to form croquette or cylinder shapes. Roll lightly in flour, dip in combined lightly beaten egg and milk, then coat with mixed breadcrumbs and parsley. Deep-fry until golden brown, drain on paper towels.
Serves 10-12

Deep-frying and roasting. *Potatoes that are to be deep-fried or roasted should always be put into hot oil or fat as this seals the outside and will prevent sogginess. The success of good deep-frying depends on clean oil being at the right temperature.*

Basic Potato Chips (French Fries)

One of the most loved and universal of all potato recipes. The ingredients couldn't be more simple but, as for all deep-frying recipes, have enough oil to half-fill your pan. Also remember to cook the chips in small batches so that they don't all clump together.

Sunflower or peanut (groundnut) oil
4 large floury potatoes
Salt and pepper

Add the oil to a warm pan and heat gently. Peel the potatoes, rinse and place in a bowl of cold water. Cut the potatoes into strips about 12 mm x 5 cm/½ x 2 inches. Put the chips into a fresh bowl of water until the oil has heated.

Roll the first batch in a clean tea-towel (dishcloth) until they are quite dry, then lower into the oil. A frying basket makes it easier to lower and raise chips in the hot oil. Cook for 5 minutes or until flabby looking, soft but not brown. Shake the basket from time to time to ensure even cooking then lift and drain.

At this stage, the chips are only partially cooked and can be set aside for several hours.

To complete cooking, reheat the oil, then plunge the chips into the hot oil to brown. This takes only 2–3 minutes.

To keep warm while individual batches are cooking, drain and place on a hot serving dish. Place in a preheated oven at 140°C/275°F/gas 1. When ready to serve, season with salt and pepper.

Serves 4

Deep-Frying Potato Chips

Cut potatoes into strips 5 cm/2 inches long x 12 mm/½ inch wide and deep.

1

Dry potato strips in a clean tea-towel (dish cloth).

2

Place potato strips in a frying basket.

3

Lower frying basket containing chips into hot oil.

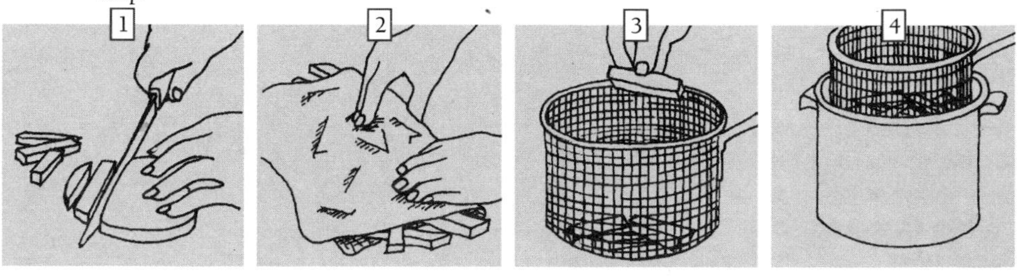

4

Herb and Potato Balls will deep-fry better if the raw ingredients are relatively dry and if they are cooked as soon as the breadcrumb process has been completed.

Herb and Potato Balls

A tasty beginning to an evening celebration.

900 g/2 lb floury potatoes
3 tablespoons mayonnaise
1 teaspoon French mustard
1 garlic clove, crushed
4 spring onions (scallions), chopped
2 tablespoons snipped chives
½ teaspoon mixed dried herbs
2 tablespoons chopped parsley
Salt and pepper
2 eggs
3 tablespoons milk
125 g/4 oz/1 cup packaged dried breadcrumbs
Oil for deep-frying

Prepare potatoes as for the mashing technique (p. 22). Add the mayonnaise and mustard and mix well. Add the garlic, onions, chives, dried herbs and parsley, and season with salt and pepper.

Roll the mixture into 2.5 cm/1 inch balls. Dip into the combined lightly beaten eggs and milk, then coat in breadcrumbs. Repeat the egg-and-breadcrumb process. Deep-fry in hot oil until golden brown.

Makes about 30

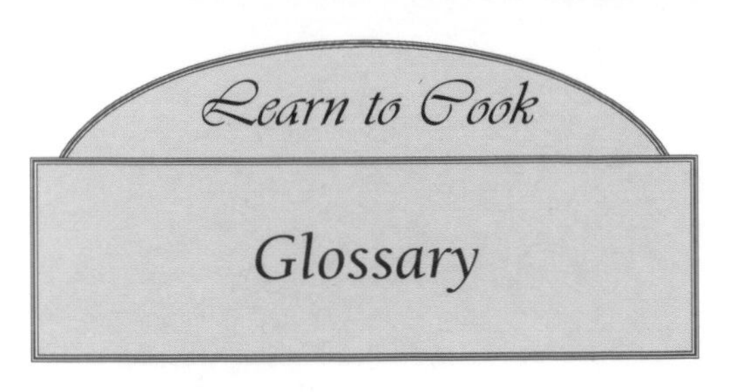

Glossary

Baking powder A mixture of chemicals based on sodium bicarbonate and cream of tartar which causes bread, cakes, scones or buns to rise during the cooking process.

Batter A cooking substance made from a mixture of flour, eggs and a liquid such as milk, water or even beer. Sweet batters sometimes contain sugar.

Clarified butter Pure butterfat, that is butter which has had the water and all non-fat solids removed. It will reach a high temperature for frying without burning.

Croquettes French for little crunchy balls or cylinders of food, rolled in egg and breadcrumbs, then deep-fried.

Desiccated coconut The dried or dehydrated pulp of the coconut palm fruit used in puddings and sweets and as an accompaniment to curries.

Dice To cut food into small cubes.

Flambé Describes food cooked or served in flaming spirits.

Ghee A form of clarified butter made from the milk of cows (and sometimes buffaloes), used in Indian cooking.

Groundnut oil Another name for peanut oil. Used for shallow- or deep-frying where extra flavour is required.

Olive oil Oil extracted from the fruit of the olive tree. The first cold-pressing extracted is termed extra virgin oil and is of the highest quality and flavour.

Paprika A mild spice powder made from the flesh (and sometimes the seeds and stalks as well) of the sweet red pepper (capsicum, bell pepper).

Parboil To boil until partly cooked.

Preheated oven An oven that has been turned on in sufficient time for it to have reached the desired temperature when you require it. Most ovens will take about 15 minutes to heat.

Purée A smooth pulp. Cooked food passed through a sieve or worked until smooth in a food processor.

Roux A mixture of butter and flour used to thicken sauces.

Sauté To cook or lightly fry food rapidly in a small amount of oil or shortening.

Simmer To cook in a liquid just under boiling point—the surface should be just trembling.

Stock Liquid made by simmering meat and vegetables in water for over three hours to extract the flavour. Used to enhance the flavour of sauces and soup.